JOSIANE FORTIN

Double Your Time

Simple Techniques to Jump-start Your Productivity

Contents

Word of Caution

Exercise sound judgment when implementing the strategies presented in this book. Your safety should always be your number one priority, and you should comply with all current laws and regulations.

The strategies I describe may not work for everyone. Remember, you are the one in control of your actions, and it is up to you to decide what is best for your unique circumstances. The information in *Double Your Time* is based on personal opinions, expertise, and experiences and may not be applicable to your situation. This book contains a collection of tips, tricks, and principles that have worked for me in different scenarios, including corporate-office, entrepreneurial, and parental settings.

The aim of this book is not to make you feel guilty or resentful about what you are not able to accomplish but rather to provide practical solutions to help you reach your goals more efficiently. Prioritize what is most important to you and align your actions with your values and aspirations.

Remember, increasing productivity is only useful if it helps you achieve your goals and create value. Use the information presented in this book to get tasks done faster so that you can have more time to enjoy the things that matter most to you.

Creating Time

Do you dream of having more time in the day to check off all the items on your to-do list? If so, I have some great news for you. I have developed a set of methods that have allowed me to double or even triple my productivity. That's right. I can get more done in one hour than most people would get done in one day. And now I want to share my secrets with you.

Over the years, I have experimented with various techniques to reach my objectives, and I am confident that the strategies outlined in this book will help you do the same. I decided to write this book to let others know about the methods available to them.

Numerous studies have shown that chronic multitaskers are not efficient, and that the brain's ability to focus decreases over time. One article in McGraw Hill Higher Education states, "Stanford University researcher Clifford Nass found that even when chronic multitaskers focused on a single task, they were less efficient. Nass concluded that over time, frequent multitasking actually changes the way the brain functions, leading to decreased productivity even when focused."[1] The article goes on to list many downsides to multitasking: it diminishes people's focus, slows them down, makes them rude, causes them to make mistakes, cuts their flow, and could be bad for the brain.

This study looked at people multitasking with their brains. Your brain can't do more than one task at a time, even if you might be able to switch quickly. For example, you might think that you are following a movie quite well while scrolling through Facebook, but you are simply switching attention.

But what if you were to combine a physical activity with a mental activity? That way, you would make use of your mind and your body instead of engaging your brain twice. Then you might just be able to complete many more tasks. For example, you could go through email while walking on a treadmill. That is the secret to multitasking the right way: combining a mindless, physical task with an intellectual pursuit.

You may be skeptical about the claim that you can double your time. Time is a finite resource that cannot be bent. However, if you can do two tasks at the same time, you are maximizing your time and getting more done. If you are doing rote activities, you might feel that you are wasting your time, but if you get two important tasks done simultaneously, you are creating more time.

I wrote this book to share my experiences and insights, with the hope that it will help you reach your goals and increase your productivity. So, let's get started and learn how to make the most of the time we have!

---

[1] https://www.mheducation.com/highered/ideas/resources-articles/multita
sking-good-or-bad-for-you

The Spark

When I landed my first full-time job after college, I quickly realized that my few hours of free time after work were mostly wasted on menial tasks like housekeeping or binge-watching TV. I felt like I was stuck in a rut. Writing a novel had always been a dream of mine, but I knew I wouldn't get it done while indulging in chips and series.

I'd been reading about productivity since my teenage years, and it was time to put that knowledge into practice with more dedication. I experimented with different techniques and implemented the ones that worked best for me. As I started getting more done, I became hooked on productivity.

My motivation was to keep the safety of a regular paycheck while still finding enough time for writing, painting, and fitness. More dreams and projects piled on from there, and now, as a wife, mother of two, and homeowner, I need to squeeze in even more activities if I want to meet my personal goals.

Over time, I've done more than I ever thought possible. My list of personal accomplishments has gotten longer. Of course, I wish I could be even further ahead, but people are often surprised when I publish another book or earn another diploma. They ask, "Where do you find the time to do all this?"

It's not always easy to pursue our dreams, but I remain

hopeful that by consistently showing up and taking small steps every day, I will get closer to crossing off all the items on my ever-growing bucket list. Even the tiniest progress in the right direction, such as sending an email, can be the turning point that leads to something greater.

Some projects require time and regular effort. Writing a book, for example, cannot be done in a single day. However, by committing to writing even just two hundred words daily, one could eventually complete a manuscript. Neglecting those small daily targets could lead to a person reaching old age without fulfilling the dream of publishing a novel. Similarly, staying fit is not achieved through a single workout but through repeated exercise over time.

When we commit to a goal and follow through, we become dependable and trustworthy individuals. Failing to respect our own commitments not only affects the specific event but also shapes our character. Neglecting a self-imposed obligation creates a bad habit that could become a pattern of behavior. For example, skipping the gym when you had planned to go not only impacts this day, but it also changes who you are. You're more likely to do it again, and then you become a slacker as you build the bad habit of not going to the gym. Therefore, it is essential to stay consistent, even when motivation is low.

Our thoughts and beliefs have a significant influence on our actions and, therefore, our own reality. If we think that we lack the time, resources, or drive to achieve something, the objective becomes harder to actualize. On the other hand, by cultivating positive emotions such as hope and perseverance, we can overcome challenges and accomplish what we set out to do. Mold yourself into someone you can trust. Do what you plan on doing. Your mind's power over your body is real, so use it.

Personally, I find hope to be a powerful motivator. It propels me out of my comfort zone and encourages me to keep going despite obstacles. Think back to a time when you persisted through adversity. What emotions sustained you?

This book is divided into two sections. In section one, you will learn tips and tricks to increase efficiency. In section two, you will explore the concept of combining activities to maximize your time.

Let's go!

Section One - Master the Basics

"When we talk about time management, it seems ridiculous to worry about speed before direction, about saving minutes when we may be wasting years." - Stephen R. Covey

Before diving into the topic of how to effectively multitask, I would like to share some productivity tips and hacks that have worked for me. I encourage you to experiment with them and assess their usefulness. Try to incorporate at least a few of them into your routine, whether for work or home. Only through trial and error can you determine how these strategies can help you reach your goals.

It is important to note that this book does not prescribe what activities are right for you. Before implementing any productivity hacks, clarify your priorities. Rushing toward a target that does not align with your values is a waste of time. To embark on a journey, you must first make sure it is the path you truly want to follow.

To create a fulfilling life, you need to have a clear vision based on your imagination and dreams. Do not merely replicate previous situations. The past does not dictate what the future holds. You have the power to start anew and pursue your dreams. Create your own blueprint for success and work toward crossing off the items on your bucket list.

Decide on your destination before heading there more quickly.

Chapter 1 - Set Priorities

Certainly, it feels great to check tasks off your to-do list, allowing you to feel proud as you lay your head down at night. However, it's easy to become overwhelmed and keep busy without direction. If you continuously run in circles, you'll go nowhere. If you run faster in the wrong direction, you'll get lost even more quickly. That's why it's crucial to establish a clear plan for your life before taking action.

Time management isn't solely about completing more tasks but is also about focusing on the ones that truly matter. To do this, you must have a firm understanding of your objectives, principles, and priorities. It's gratifying to see tangible results but only if they align with your life vision. If you don't remain mindful of your goals, you may find yourself agreeing to solve someone else's urgent issues or accepting random invitations, leaving you no time to tackle the most important tasks. Stay focused and don't let distractions sidetrack you.

It's common for people to fill their schedules haphazardly, without a plan or intention, reacting to whatever life throws their way. They may believe that staying busy is a prerequisite for success or worthiness, but this is a fallacy that can lead to burnout and discontent.

Instead of attempting to do everything, concentrate on the

activities that are most meaningful to you. Ensure that your schedule aligns with your aspirations and don't hesitate to decline offers that are not worthwhile. It's easy to become consumed by the busyness of life and overlook what truly matters to you.

Your life vision may change over time. For instance, you may shift from desiring a lavish home and car at age twenty to wanting a large family at age thirty and perhaps a simpler, off-the-grid lifestyle at age forty. All these visions are valid, but they necessitate different approaches. If you recognize that your vision has evolved, adjust your actions accordingly.

Attempting to do more things that lack significance won't help you live your best life. Instead, it will distract you from what truly matters.

Chapter 2 - Decide

To save time and take more action, it's critical to avoid indecision. Choices can be made in a matter of seconds. Although certain decisions may require some fact-finding, in my experience, "trying to decide" is usually just a form of procrastination fueled by fear of choosing badly. However, there is no such thing as a wrong decision. Each one advances you, even the so-called bad ones. When you refuse to decide, you remain where you are, and there is no room for growth or improvement.

This is particularly true for small, daily decisions. For instance, don't waste time reading an email and then setting it aside because you're uncertain about the next course of action. Be decisive. Determine the next step and execute it right away: reply, forward, or delete the message. If you don't have the time to act immediately, don't read the email. Why would you want to read an email multiple times when you already receive too many of them?

Another aspect of being a more decisive person is taking advantage of opportunities without overthinking the possibility of failure. For example, imagine you'd like to increase people's recognition of your expertise in a certain area. An old friend contacts you to offer a speaking engagement during a webinar he is organizing at work. Would you accept? Many people would decline this opportunity, claiming they are not ready or are experiencing imposter syndrome. In contrast, a decisive person would quickly recognize that this opportunity aligns with their vision, say yes, then figure it out along the way. Don't deprive yourself of opportunities.

I like to think of myself as someone who doesn't say no to opportunities. Whenever I come across a job posting that interests me, I send my résumé. When there is a call for projects, I fill out the application. If there is a writing contest, I submit my short story. While they may say no to me, I won't say no to myself. I don't want to regret missing out on an opportunity and wonder if I could have received a positive response. I know I've given it my all.

Over time, I've learned that receiving negative responses gets easier. In the past, a rejection could halt my progress for a week or more, leaving me feeling ashamed for even trying. But now it only stings for about four seconds, and then I'm back on track. If what I had to offer wasn't a good fit, it doesn't mean I'm worthless. Perhaps the timing wasn't right. So, what's next?

Moreover, I've gained many opportunities and jobs by stepping out of my comfort zone. I've celebrated many successes as a result of this approach.

Deciding means taking control of your life and shaping it according to your desires. If you don't decide, the default choice has been made, and you are not leading a deliberate life. Many projects stall due to indecision. Making up your mind about something and sticking with it is one of the most important things you can do with your brain. The minutes you spend being unsure about the next step are stealing your dreams away. Take the time to find the answer within your mind. Identifying what you want is essential to achieving it. This will allow you to move forward and get things done.

There is a saying: "It's better to ask for forgiveness than permission." Deciding is not only the first step to acting, but it also frees up mental power. Your brain won't waste energy looping the same question.

So, what decisions should you be making today?

Chapter 3 - Plan Your Year

Based on the priorities you have established, you should have a clearer vision for your life. What are the key areas you want to work on this year to make that a reality? What specific actions do you need to take on a day-to-day basis? Are you someone who can focus on one project for a couple of months before switching to another, or do you prefer to work on multiple projects at once?

Conventional wisdom suggests that working on one thing at a time is the most efficient way to make progress. However, this approach doesn't work for everyone. Some people, me included, thrive on variety and find that working on several projects at once keeps us engaged. In my experience, trying to focus on a single activity can lead to boredom and distractibility, which slows progress. Therefore, I have found a balance that works for me: having four or five projects a year that I can move back and forth between, according to my mood and motivation level.

If you're someone who enjoys variety, you might also prefer working on multiple projects at once, even if it means taking longer to complete each one. The key is to know yourself and experiment with different approaches. I've written a book called *The One-Year Plan* that's specifically designed for people with many interests, which you might find helpful.

Regardless of your working style, it's important to set clear objectives for the year and schedule times to work on them. Review your progress every month to stay on track. What projects are you making good progress on? What's not working? Are there new tasks you should add to your list to move you closer to your personal or career goals? And don't be afraid to revise your objectives if your priorities change or life throws you a curveball. Planning should be a flexible and dynamic process that evolves with you.

Chapter 4 - Plan Your Week

Once you have a vision for your life and have identified what you want to work on for the year, it's important to break down those ambitious plans into smaller steps that can be completed in short periods of time. The best way to do this is by scheduling a weekly planning session.

During this planning session, review the status of your current projects, update your to-do list and calendar, and check for upcoming deadlines, meetings, and training. Ask yourself: "At the end of this week, what actions do I want to have completed?"

I used to take an hour for this planning session, but now I find that thirty minutes is sufficient. Breaking down a project into manageable chunks can be challenging, but remember the saying: "How do you eat an elephant? One bite at a time."

If you're unsure of what needs to be done next, try brainstorming. For example, you might think, "I could start by talking to Sam," which could lead to the realization that you need information from Jack first, which leads you to send an email to Jack. This thought process helps you generate possibilities and get unstuck.

Each task should be a specific action that can take anywhere from five to sixty minutes to complete. Examples could be calling a consultant to schedule an appointment, writing three hundred words, or sending a business proposal to five prospects. It's important to know when a task is considered complete. If a task takes less than five minutes to finish, it's best to get it done right away. This prevents small tasks from adding up and becoming a distraction.

If you work closely with others, you should briefly meet with them to follow up on project progress. When you're well organized, you only need to glance at your action list to make this meeting last less than ten minutes.

Chapter 5 - Plan Your Day

The best time to plan for tomorrow is today. Before your workday is over, take a few minutes to review your to-do list and mark off any completed or canceled tasks. Also, check your agenda for the following day to get a sense of what to expect when you get back to the office. This will allow you to plan accordingly and prepare documents or dress appropriately for an important meeting. Additionally, reviewing your calendar can help you avoid any surprises, like a doctor's appointment in the middle of the day that you may have forgotten about. This daily review ensures that you are prepared rather than caught off guard.

At the end of the day, determine the top three tasks that you must complete the next day to move closer to your most important life goals. Doing this before leaving the office is ideal as you are still thinking about what needs to be done and familiar with your priorities. Moreover, it's easier to commit to difficult activities since you don't have to do them until the next day. You won't have the extra burden of your mind telling you that you don't feel like doing them. This is particularly beneficial for those who tend to procrastinate.

One advantage of this method is that you can start working right away when you get to your desk since your to-do list tells you exactly what needs to be done first. There is no need to make decisions as you have already made them in advance.

Sometimes, even the simplest chores—such as making a phone call or a doing quick web search—can shift you closer to your goals. Make sure you have enough time to complete those tasks. Try to schedule them when you typically have the most energy and your brain is primed. Although it may not always be possible to use these ideal time slots, you can start protecting them by scheduling meetings at other times.

At the end of each day, evaluate what you have accomplished. This should only take a couple of minutes if you set it up properly. Superperformers regularly review their progress to ensure that they are moving forward. You can't measure up if you don't measure your data.

Various key performance indicators (KPIs) can be used to measure performance, some directly and some indirectly. Consider the example of a salesperson. While sales revenue is a commonly used KPI, it is not entirely under the salesperson's control. External factors such as customer mood, product quality, and pricing can all affect sales. This makes sales an indirect result of the salesperson's efforts.

A more direct indicator of a salesperson's performance would be their input. For example, how many prospecting calls did they make each week? Input KPIs are under the salesperson's control, whereas output KPIs depend on how others react to their actions.

In the case of an author, sales data is an indirect KPI, while word count is a direct KPI. The author has direct control over the number of words written and published and can take action to increase or decrease it. However, sales data is not entirely under the author's control, even though it is influenced by the author's actions.

When it comes to success in any field, focusing on both the quality and quantity of specific inputs is crucial. However, increasing the quantity of input alone can also improve the quality, as practice and repetition can help individuals achieve excellence.

For instance, a salesperson who regularly makes numerous prospecting calls each week, even if they initially struggle to communicate the value of the product, will improve with experience. Over time, they will become more confident and effective in their communication, ultimately leading to more conversions and sales.

Similarly, for an author, increasing the number of published books may not necessarily result in more sales. However, by writing more, they can improve their craft and hone their storytelling skills, leading to the creation of more compelling and engaging books that appeal to a wider audience.

By investing time and effort in improving the quantity of specific inputs each day, people can increase the probability of achieving their goals. As they strive to produce more and higher-quality work, they will inevitably become more skilled and successful in their respective fields. Ultimately, a commitment to consistent practice and improvement is key to reaching one's full potential.

Chapter 6 - Lower Your Standards

I t's time to let go of some of the unrealistic expectations that we place on ourselves and lower our standards. The pressure to be perfect all the time can be overwhelming and exhausting, and it's time to give ourselves a break. We need to remind ourselves that our lives are not Instagram threads, and we don't need to meet unrealistic standards. Forget about having a spotless home twenty-four, seven.

Start by cutting yourself some slack. Not every task deserves to be done to perfection, and it's okay to simplify things. Take the example of a kid's birthday party. Do you really need to invite fifteen friends for your child to be happy? Does the decorating need to be elaborate? Who are you trying to impress with themed invitations, complicated menus, ice sculptures, mascots, and tarot readings? Keep the party much more basic. You'll save time, money, and the environment, and your kid will still love it. And your kid's joy is the whole point of the party.

For those of us who struggle to keep a tidy house, there are a few hacks we can use. For instance, when folding laundry, we don't have to fold our underwear. We can stash them in a basket in our drawer. We can also clean the dishes once a week, including pots and pans, and skip the rinsing. These practices may seem shameful, but it's okay to keep them to ourselves and not worry about what others may think. It'll be our secret.

You can also let go of the need to iron or buy complicated clothes that require dry cleaning. Simplify your makeup routine or get rid of it altogether. By doing so, you can free up time to focus on things that truly matter to you, such as working on your legacy.

By lowering our standards and simplifying our lives, we can find more time and energy to pursue our passions and invest in the things that bring us joy and fulfillment. It's time to let go of perfectionism and embrace a more relaxed way of living.

What are some areas where you could be experimenting with lower expectations?

Chapter 7 - Automate Tasks

Why waste your time on tasks that a computer program can easily handle? Automating tasks can save you significant time and effort while also reducing the risk of human error and ensuring greater accuracy and consistency. In addition, automation can help you scale your work more efficiently, giving you the freedom to focus on more creative and high-value tasks.

To get started with automation, be creative. Look at your recurring tasks and identify those that are repetitive or time-consuming. Experiment with new tools and processes to discover faster ways of completing your work, and be ruthless about cutting those that don't add value.

For instance, if you find yourself giving the same answers repeatedly, it can be a huge time-saver to create a page with answers to frequently asked questions. This can be especially useful if you have a business or a website that receives a lot of customer inquiries or if you communicate often with clients, colleagues, or partners. The FAQ page becomes a great resource for your customers. They can find answers to common questions without having to contact you. It is faster for them and you.

For other types of questions, you might want to create email templates. Start by identifying the common questions or requests you receive. Then create a prewritten response. You can create multiple templates for different types of inquiries or requests and customize them as needed. By using email templates, you can answer more quickly and ensure that you are providing consistent and accurate information.

During one of my jobs, I often received requests from customers to send the same files repeatedly. To save time and effort, I created a folder on my desktop specifically for these files. With just one click, I could attach a document to an email without having to search for it. It was not automation per se, but it still goes to show how it is possible to simplify recurring processes. This is just one example of how you can streamline your work. By implementing automation strategies like these, you can save time and increase your productivity.

Have you ever thought about creating a spreadsheet that can quickly generate tables that you have to build each month? When you need to create reports with data, make sure you have built tools that allow you to update everything in a matter of minutes. Your colleagues will be amazed at how fast you can churn out information week after week.

When gathering information, why not use tools like Google Forms or Survey Monkey? These apps take care of building reports out of the data. If people won't answer surveys, you can fill them out yourself based on the answers they give you over the phone. In the end, you get the data all nice and pretty.

You can automate decisions as well. Decision fatigue can prevent you from acting, so reduce the number of choices you have to make in a day. Some tasks recur in my calendar, so I don't need to decide when to do them. I know I work out during lunch. I know I back up my files once a month. There is no decision to make—it's automatic. What tasks keep showing up in your daily or weekly schedule?

Meal planning is another area where automation can be useful. Some people have the same meal every single Monday, while others order from meal-subscription services.

Here's a tip for filling up the dishwasher: sort the short plates from the big ones. It doesn't take more time, but when you empty the dishwasher, you can easily grab up to four plates with one hand and place them in the cupboard. You can empty the dishwasher in a couple of minutes in the morning while your bread is toasting. Most importantly, nobody will have an excuse to leave dishes on the counter, because the dishwasher will be empty.

Automating regular payments is a simple, effective way to streamline your financial management. Many companies offer the option to charge your credit card automatically, with only occasional monitoring required to ensure that there are no mistakes or surcharges. Personally, I review my credit card and bank transactions once a month with a two-minute glance. Sending a predetermined amount to your savings accounts is another effortless way to manage your finances. Set it and forget it!

Finally, automating activities is another excellent way to utilize the autopilot function. We can compile a list of tasks that can be automated in our personal or professional lives, such as prefilling forms with recurring information, simplifying work processes by removing redundant activities, standard-izing repetitive tasks, and suggesting process improvements. Although automating tasks may require some effort initially, it saves us time and energy in the long run.

Overall, automating tasks and decisions is a smart way

to optimize your workflow, improve your productivity, and achieve more in less time.

Chapter 8 - Manage Your Energy Levels

Have you noticed how your energy levels can vary throughout the day, the week, and even the year? It's essential to identify your most productive time slots and use them wisely. Are you a morning person, or do you feel more energetic at night when the kids are asleep? Do you feel sluggish in the afternoon? By checking how you feel, you can notice trends and plan accordingly.

I have come to know when I have the most—and the least—energy. Therefore, when I plan my activities, I take this information into consideration. For instance, I've identified that Monday is my most productive day. After a weekend break, I feel refreshed and determined to succeed in the new week. Knowing this, I schedule tasks that require the most focus, determination, or strategy, such as making important phone calls, writing, or fixing something around the house. On Mondays, I often feel unstoppable, crossing off tasks on my to-do list at lightning speed. I regularly get all my most important tasks of the week done on Monday.

On Saturdays, I prioritize housecleaning and cooking. It is not unusual to have the dishwasher, the washer, and the dryer all working by the time my kids are eating breakfast.

Generally, my brain is most alert in the morning, and its activity slows down as the day progresses. However, I've noticed that it comes back around nine at night. If I have urgent tasks, I use this window to get them done. For example, I take care of university coursework or writing during this time.

Although I used to be a night owl, my routine changed due to kids and work, and I adjusted my lifestyle accordingly. As I had to wake up earlier, I had no choice but to go to bed earlier too. I decided to make the best out of this new lifestyle. At one point, I was exercising in the morning before work, but as I now work from home, I've switched things up again to do it during my lunchtime. Adapt to life changes.

Right now, identify your most alert and energetic times during the day and week and make sure you schedule your critical activities for when you feel most productive.

Chapter 9 - List It

I recommend that you take the time to write down a plan. This will help you attack each project with confidence and clarity. When you create a list, you're deciding what needs to be done. By doing this ahead of time, you won't waste time during work, wondering what to do next.

While many people believe their minds are powerful enough to juggle everything, a brain doesn't function efficiently that way. Don't use your precious brainpower to store floating ideas that may pop up at any time of the day. Instead, clear your mind by writing everything down.

Start by listing your current projects. Then figure out what the next steps are. It could be just the one, or it could be a full list of tasks. Let's use the example of renovating a bathroom. Where do you start? The first actions could be to research local interior designers, select one, call to make an appointment, and then attend the appointment. Once those tasks are done, you will be able to determine what the next steps are to complete the renovation.

List precise steps that are easy to accomplish. For instance, renovating a bathroom may feel overwhelming, but making an appointment is simple. You're more likely to get things done if they feel easy. You trick your brain into action and steer away from procrastination.

Also, by breaking big projects into short tasks, you can make use of small time slots. For example, if you know that writing emails is the next step, you can send three of them while waiting at the doctor's office. There are always pockets of time you can steal during the day—during your break at work, during lunch, or while your kids nap. You could use a daily walk to do a live recording for social media or to record a podcast.

Once you have your list, insert the items into your calendar and discipline yourself to stick to your plan. I've found that having a task on my calendar makes me more likely to complete it, even if I don't want to do it. Although you may not know exactly how much time each step will take, you should have an approximate idea. Give yourself a reasonable but inflexible timeframe, hold yourself accountable to finish within the allotted time, and your mind will be laser focused on each task.

You may be familiar with Parkinson's Law, which states that "work expands so as to fill the time available for its completion." If you give yourself two weeks to write a blog post, you'll be tempted to wait until the last hour to start working on it. Instead, schedule an hour in your calendar right now, and you'll avoid agonizing over the post for two weeks.

Previously, at work, I would write the project name in pen and list all the next steps I could take alongside it, on the same line. I would then prioritize them by assigning a number to each line. Once I handed off the project to someone else, it would fall out of my list until it was returned to me. I would cross off items as I completed them and update the list as I went along.

However, my work situation has changed. I now set aside a small amount of time on Mondays to write down all the tasks I want to accomplish during the week and then add them to my calendar. When I lack motivation, I can turn to my calendar and force myself to tackle what has already been scheduled.

The most important thing is to have a specific outcome in mind so you know what steps you must do. Actions listed should be specific. When you read a line, you should know exactly what action to do:

- Call John to follow up on the proposal.
- Find three suppliers of cardboard boxes and call them to get estimates.
- Write 250 words for the newsletter.

Be specific. "Get sales" would be too vague. Instead, you could write, "Call three prospects."

Overall, maintaining effective to-do lists, whether on paper or in your digital calendar, can help you optimize your productivity and ensure that you are always in the right place at the right time.

Chapter 10 - Bundle

Even the most productive of us have tasks we'd rather avoid but which still need to be done. Whether it's making phone calls or running errands, these activities can be time-consuming and stressful, especially when squeezed into an already packed schedule. One solution is to bundle similar tasks together. Let's explore this concept further.

The most obvious benefit of bundling is that it is efficient. When you do similar activities within the same timeframe, you don't have to switch from one task to the next throughout the day, so you maintain your focus. This will save you time overall—time that could be used more productively elsewhere. Also, bundling helps with organization because it forces you to keep track of your tasks.

If you, like many others, dread calling people to make appointments or following up with clients, consider grouping these tasks together. Instead of making calls throughout the week, schedule a specific time in your calendar to complete all your phone calls at once. This will not only save you time but also reduce the number of times you experience anxiety about making calls.

Another helpful bundling tip is to create itemized lists for each type of errand. The best way to manage this is to write down what you need the second you think about it. You need to set up a system for this. For example, when I notice that we need more eggs, I add it right away to the list. You can use apps like Google Keep to share your lists with family members, making it easier to remember items and coordinate shopping trips. This way, you won't rely on your memory, and you'll prevent unnecessary trips or duplicate purchases.

In addition to bundling, I try to match my errands with other activities. For example, if I'm visiting a friend, I might pick up some items at the drugstore on the way. The list can help with this. By keeping it updated, I can trust that I won't forget anything I need.

Another way to save time is by ordering online. This can be especially helpful for items that you regularly use or that are difficult to find in stores.

With some planning ahead and minor adjustments to your routine, you can keep things running smoothly and avoid unnecessary stress. Try bundling to streamline your day. You may be pleasantly surprised by how much easier life becomes.

Chapter 11 - Focus Time

anaging multiple projects can be challenging and distracting, so you should focus on one of them at a time. Complete as much of one as possible before moving on to the next. Even if many tasks are calling at once, having an efficient workflow can help you ensure that you're on top of everything.

One way to do this is by dedicating specific blocks of uninterrupted time—focus time—to completing tasks. Break down large ones into manageable chunks, and then allocate a specific block of time for each. When scheduling your tasks, consider their importance and urgency as well as your energy levels. For example, if you know you have more motivation in the morning, place the most difficult tasks in the morning and keep the easiest for the afternoon. The key to maximizing your focus time is to plan.

Of course, it's also important to be flexible and make adjustments as necessary. If someone is waiting for a response from you, set aside time to follow up with them. Just be sure to set boundaries and not let others take over your planning or encroach on your priorities.

In my experience working at a large company, it's common to wait for others' input as you move forward with a project.

This can involve getting approval from colleagues, following up with suppliers, requesting data from coworkers, or awaiting feedback from a committee. My favorite thing is to ensure that the work I have stays as little on my desk as possible. I answer all emails the day I receive them. I get tasks done quickly so they can wait on my boss's desk for approval or get moved to another department. That way, my desk remains free of clutter, and I can focus on other tasks.

During meetings, avoid multitasking or answering emails on your phone. That's not efficient, and it's rude anyway. Instead, make the most of the opportunity to contribute to team efforts. Whenever possible, switch to online meetings to save time and money. If you can avoid attending meetings altogether, even better.

Focus time is an essential part of managing multiple projects at once while still getting everything done efficiently. Planning focus time is the foundation of my day, allowing me to pursue many of my dreams. Try it for yourself!

Chapter 12 - Manage Distractions

We've all been there—sitting at a desk, determined to focus and get some work done, only to be distracted by a colleague who wants to share the latest office gossip. While chatting with colleagues is important for building relationships and enhancing your presence in the office, it's crucial to strike a balance between socializing and getting things done. Office politics can help you advance in the corporate world, but don't waste the whole day talking. Additionally, if you find yourself constantly being approached by colleagues who need to vent or converse excessively, it's important to set boundaries and be strategic about your interactions. If you're stuck at your desk with a chatty colleague, try getting up and walking with them while you chat, then make your exit when you reach their desk.

You also need to know how to say no to things that don't align with your vision. When politely declining an offer or request from a colleague or client, explain why their offer doesn't fit into your plan and move forward. Don't worry about offending anyone. Just be honest and straightforward about what works best for you.

If you find yourself constantly sidetracked by emails, social media activity, and text messages, it may be helpful to turn off notifications or even internet access. Eliminating these distractions can help you stay focused. To stay motivated during tedious tasks, try rewarding yourself with something enjoyable after a certain amount of time. For example, you could allow yourself fifteen minutes of social media or video browsing after completing forty-five minutes of work. Experiment with different time ratios to find what works best for you, but be sure to stick to your allotted reward time. In addition to helping you complete your work, taking regular breaks throughout the day can help refresh your mind.

Managing distractions takes practice and discipline, but with these strategies in mind, it should become easier to stay focused and productive throughout the day.

Chapter 13 - Take Action

The concept of procrastination is ridiculous. So much precious time is wasted simply because we just can't get ourselves to act. Procrastination often stems from uncertainty about what to do next, which can be paralyzing. But why should we let procrastination rule our lives when there is so much we could be accomplishing? Though it can seem easier to just stay where you are rather than venture into unknown territory, if you want to get anything done, you have to step out of your state of indecision.

The first step in overcoming procrastination is taking control of your projects list. Decide which items you can act on without waiting for input from others. If there are tasks that require actions from other people, why not follow up on them? That way, you won't have to wait around for someone else to act before you start working on something.

If you're feeling stuck, ask your boss for direction, do a Google search for step-by-step guides, or seek help from colleagues who may have relevant expertise or experience. There are many resources available. Don't let yourself become overwhelmed—break each task down into manageable chunks and start working on one piece at a time. You are resourceful. Figure it out.

Challenge yourself to tackle tasks that intimidate you, even if they appear too difficult or complicated. Get them off your plate. This can lead to a great sense of satisfaction. Starting is usually the toughest part, but as you progress, a task becomes easier until it no longer feels like work.

Don't be afraid to request help. Whether it's seeking assistance from a colleague, making a sales pitch, or requesting resources, don't shy away from asking. The worst that can happen is to be told no. While rejection can be discouraging at first, it becomes more manageable with each instance, and the wins you achieve make it worthwhile.

Rather than waiting for the perfect opportunity to work on a project, take advantage of any available pockets of time, no matter how small. We are often interrupted and distracted throughout the day. People tend to think that they need a large block of uninterrupted time in order to be productive, but this is not always possible in the real world.

Waiting for the ideal conditions to present themselves can lead to procrastination and decreased productivity. Instead, use small amounts of unclaimed time, even if it's only ten minutes between meetings, to review a report, respond to emails, or make a quick phone call. You can accomplish more than you might think. This strategy can help you keep yourself on track and avoid getting bogged down by the desire for the ideal conditions.

Don't be afraid to tackle the hard stuff—in fact, make it a priority. Don't fear failure. It is a natural part of the road to success, and if you're not making mistakes, you're not trying hard enough.

By taking control of your projects list and seeking help when necessary, you can overcome feelings of being overwhelmed and take positive steps toward completing your goals.

Instead of worrying about the unknown, we can conquer our fears and take control of our own destinies. Each of us has unlimited potential—all we need to do is tap into it. With some effort, everyone can make progress toward their objectives and feel proud of moving forward.

Don't wait any longer—do what you know you should be doing!

Chapter 14 - Organize Your Space

There are several reasons why organizing your workspace is crucial. Firstly, a chaotic workspace can be distracting and make it challenging to focus on tasks, leading to decreased productivity, whereas a clean, tidy workspace enables you to work more efficiently.

Secondly, a well-organized workspace allows you to locate tools and materials easily, saving time and reducing the frustration of searching for items. This can boost productivity by allowing you to focus on the task at hand.

Thirdly, a cluttered workspace can be visually overwhelming and inhibit your ability to think creatively. An organized workspace can help you clear your mind and boost your creativity by providing a more relaxing and inspiring environment.

Lastly, a messy workspace can cause stress and make you feel overwhelmed. By organizing your workspace, you can create a more calming and stress-free environment, which can improve your overall well-being and help you get more done.

Therefore, organizing your workspace is essential for productivity and efficiency. But how can you achieve it? There are several steps you can take to create a more structured workspace.

Firstly, identify what tools, materials, and equipment you

need to work effectively. Keep the items you use most often within arm's reach, and store less frequently used items in drawers or other designated areas. Get rid of the things you seldom use. Avoid overstocking your workspace with unnecessary office supplies and only keep what you need. If you have fifteen pens, you need to search each time to find the one you like. Keep only the one you like and maybe a backup one. This way, you'll quickly locate what you need.

For instance, I have set up a small art workshop in my home, where I paint. Whenever I feel creative, I don't have to waste time rummaging through a crowded closet to find my tools. Instead, I can go to my workspace, where everything is set in place, and get started. Moreover, I don't have to put it all back in the closet when I'm done.

Secondly, maintain a clean and clutter-free desk. A disorganized workspace can be distracting and impede your ability to concentrate. Take a few minutes at the end of each day to discard any items you no longer need. Periodically wipe down surfaces, toss out trash, and put away tools and materials you're finished with. Sitting down at a tidy desk can be an inviting start to the day.

Also, make sure you are comfortable. An ergonomic workspace will help you prevent injuries and maintain productivity. Adjust your chair, keyboard, and screen to suit your needs. If you're right-handed, answer the phone with your left hand and take notes with the right.

Avoid printing documents whenever possible. Keep files on your computer and create shortcuts to frequently used folders. Develop a naming and filing system that is easy to understand and use the search function as a backup. The best system should be so self-evident that anyone replacing you would quickly understand it. If you need to sign documents, use the free version of Adobe Acrobat to do that electronically.

Finally, make sure to have a backup system in place to protect your work. Add this to your list as a recurring task, and regularly backup your files to ensure that you never lose important data—or even better, have it done automatically.

By implementing these tips and creating an organized workspace, you'll save time and energy, which can lead to increased productivity and better results.

Chapter 15 - Use Autopilot

The autopilot function of our brain is an incredible ability that we can harness to improve our productivity and streamline our lives. By understanding how the brain works, we can find ways to use its natural tendencies to our advantage.

One way to do this is to perform certain tasks frequently. Through the process of repetition, the brain creates a pathway that makes it easier to do this task in the future. For example, if you want to start driving to the gym instead of driving home, you can create a new pathway in your brain by making that detour repeatedly. Over time, this new pathway becomes stronger and more ingrained, making it easier to get to the gym.

Another way we can use the autopilot function is to be mindful of our current habits and patterns. Once we recognize the things we do on a daily basis without even thinking about them, we can begin to make positive changes. By identifying the habits we desire, we can create new neural pathways that support our goals. For instance, if I'm in the habit of brushing my teeth every morning, I can place my sunscreen next to my toothbrush to remind me to apply it too. We can intentionally build a habit through association and repetition.

Another way to use the autopilot function is to create a system of reminders and cues that trigger specific actions. For example, if we want to start drinking more water throughout the day, we can create a cue, such as a phone alert or a sticky note. This cue can trigger our autopilot function to regularly remind us to drink water.

One of the most significant benefits of using the autopilot function is that mental space is freed up for more critical tasks. When we can perform routine tasks automatically, we don't have to devote as much thought to them, allowing us to focus on more complex or creative tasks. This can increase our productivity and enhance our problem-solving abilities.

Additionally, we can use the autopilot function to our advantage by practicing mindfulness and meditation. By training the brain to be more present in the moment, we can enhance our ability to remain focused and attentive.

While the autopilot function can be incredibly useful, we should also be cautious about relying too heavily on it. We need to remain present and aware of our surroundings, especially when doing activities that require our full attention, such as driving or operating machinery.

The autopilot function of the brain is an incredible ability that we can harness to improve our productivity and streamline our lives. By deliberately training the brain, being mindful of our habits and patterns, automating tasks, creating systems of reminders and cues, and practicing mindfulness and meditation, we can use the autopilot function to our advantage.

Chapter 16 - Be Consistent

Setting and achieving goals is an essential part of personal and professional growth. However, many people struggle with sticking to their plans. This is where consistency comes in.

Consistency is the act of showing up and putting in the work day after day, even when you are tired or not in the mood. It's the practice of doing something regularly until it becomes a habit. Consistency is the key to success, and it applies to all areas of life, from health and fitness to career—or individual and family—objectives.

One way to be consistent is to break down your goals into manageable tasks. This can help you stay focused and motivated. This way, you'll be able to track your progress and see how far you've come.

For example, if your goal is to write a book, start by setting a plan to write five hundred words a day. This may seem like a small effort, but eventually, those five hundred words will add up. By the end of the year, you'll have written over 180,000 words. That's a book!

Another way to be consistent is to make it easy to start. Leave your gym bag close to the door so you're ready to work out when you wake up. Set up a workspace for your crafts so you're ready to start creating when you have some free time. By making it easy to start, you remove any excuses that may hold you back.

It can also be helpful to establish routines. For example, if you want to exercise regularly, set a specific time and day for your workouts. This will help you stay on track.

Accountability can also be a powerful motivator. Find a friend or family member who shares your goals and check in with them regularly. Having someone to hold you accountable can help you stay motivated.

Though consistency isn't always easy, it's worth it. Research has shown that those who are steady are more likely to reach their goals than those who only put in sporadic effort. By staying consistent, you build trust with yourself and others. You learn to rely on yourself and your ability to stick with a plan.

Consistency is the key to success. By setting small, doable tasks for yourself, making it easy to start, establishing routines, and finding an accountability partner, you can achieve your goals. Remember, little steps add up to big results.

Chapter 17 - Challenge Yourself

Remember Parkinson's Law from chapter nine? It says that work expands so as to fill the time available for its completion. You need to face your beliefs about how long a task should take and challenge yourself to innovate. Look at your processes and be creative. Find shortcuts.

Try to find new ways of doing things faster while still maintaining high quality. Think outside the box—brainstorm new ideas with colleagues and test out different approaches until you find something that works best for you and your team.

Make sure that you are not simply pretending to be busy. Stop doing busywork. Not only is it a waste of time, but it doesn't add any value to the real work you might be doing. Ask yourself if an activity is necessary or if there are ways of getting the same result in less time. If a task isn't necessary, then don't do it—this will help you save energy for more important tasks. Identify which tasks add value and which don't. This means taking an honest look at yourself and reflecting on how you are spending your time.

I have seen so many reports sent up the ladder that were jam-packed with information, when all the boss wanted was a couple of key indicators. If a report or document contains information that no one is using, then why include it? Asking questions helps ensure that everyone is on the same page regarding expectations—and ultimately saves everyone from scrambling at the last minute because something wasn't clear from the start.

Sometimes, top management doesn't know what they want until they see a first report, but don't assume that everything you suggested is necessary. Check with the report owner about what is useful and scrap the rest. Remember that times change—people change their minds or change jobs. Make sure that all the tasks you do add value and are not busywork.

Challenging yourself when it comes to managing time is essential for achieving success in any profession or project. It allows you to think critically about how much time certain activities should take, eliminating busywork and unnecessary data from reports and documents, and brainstorming with colleagues about how best to complete tasks efficiently while still maintaining high standards. All these efforts can lead to greater productivity overall, so start challenging yourself today!

Chapter 18 - Give Up

In today's world, it's easy to get caught up in the frenzy of having it all, doing it all, and being it all. Social media, advertising, and the pressure to succeed can make us feel like we need to accomplish everything all at once. But we are only human, and we have limitations.

If you are like me and have a million projects and dreams, you know it's impossible to do them all at once. Instead of just pushing yourself until you're burned out, you could temporarily give up on some so that you can focus on the ones that matter most. Whether it's our health, relationships, career, or personal growth, we need to give our attention to the areas that matter most to us. By doing this, we can be more productive, fulfilled, and successful.

The first step is determining which of your projects are the most important. It's okay to focus on the ones that are the most meaningful or beneficial for your life right now. Don't be afraid to postpone undertakings for later. This doesn't mean that they won't ever get done—it just means they won't get done right away. We are putting them on hold until a more appropriate time. We can revisit them when we have more time, energy, or resources to dedicate to them. We should keep our goals and dreams in mind, but we also need to be flexible and adapt to changing circumstances and priorities.

One way to prioritize is by creating a timeline with a clear target to work toward. Take a look at your list of projects and determine which ones need to be completed first and which can wait until later. This will help you stay organized and make sure that everything gets done eventually—or at least when it needs to be done. Plus, having a timeline will help keep you motivated by showing you exactly what needs to be done next.

Make an honest assessment of what you can realistically accomplish and set boundaries for yourself. There is just no way you can do it all, because if you are like me, the number of things you want to do is infinite. If I just think of all the books and movie scripts I would like to write, I know that I would never be able to finish them all in one year. I get more ideas every day! And that's just one aspect of my life. I have kids to raise, paintings to create, a house to keep, renovations to finish, political actions to engage in, another degree to get... and a full-time job. This means that I must prioritize my undertakings and give some of them up until another time. Some I will eventually get to. Some I will lose interest in. I wrote a whole book about prioritizing the projects for a year: *The One-Year Plan*.

It's natural to want to pursue all our dreams simultaneously. However, the truth is that we cannot achieve everything at once. To prevent burnout and maximize our chances of success, we need to focus on a select few projects at a time and complete them before moving on to others.

Chapter 19 - Solve Your Personal Problems

L ife is filled with challenges, and it can feel like we are constantly battling worries and issues. But we don't have to just endure them. Focusing on our personal issues at work can cloud our minds and affect us in negative ways. Therefore, it's important to manage our personal lives and prevent problems from arising in the first place.

While there is no way to be completely free of issues, you can take steps to reduce the burden. Taking care of yourself is crucial for living a happy and fulfilling life, and it can help you avoid many issues altogether. Some simple actions you can take include eating well, exercising, spending quality time with your family, managing your finances responsibly, having hobbies, getting enough sleep, and staying hydrated.

However, depending on your personality, you may find other activities more helpful in reducing the impact of personal problems. For example, some people enjoy meditating, taking walks in nature, doing breathwork, journaling, or talking to a life coach or therapist. Whatever helps you feel good and lowers your stress levels, integrate it into your daily routine.

Taking care of yourself is not always easy, but it's essential for living a happy life. By taking proactive steps to prevent issues from affecting our work lives, you can increase your productivity in the long run. The point is that you must be healthy, happy, and energized to get things done. Do your best to be at your best.

Chapter 20 - Keep on Learning

It's important to continue learning and investing in yourself as you build your career. No matter where you are in your career, there is always something more to learn. Let's explore why continuous learning is so beneficial.

If you want to be more successful at work, try learning what other departments do. Having a better understanding of how each department functions helps create a cohesive workplace. This will also give you a greater sense of appreciation for each person's unique role within the organization. Plus, the more knowledge you have about the company, the better equipped you will be to make decisions that benefit everyone involved.

Keep learning in your field of interest, but don't be afraid to take courses outside of your knowledge base. Taking classes of any kind can provide valuable insight and inspiration for projects or tasks at work. Even if these courses don't directly relate to what you do on a daily basis, it never hurts to expand your horizons with things that interest you.

Another way of learning is to take on tasks or jobs that are unfamiliar to you. Don't let fear get in the way of an opportunity just because it's outside of what you know how to do—you will learn! There is much more value in trying something new than in saying no. Attempting something different also prepares you for future encounters with similar opportunities so that the next time around, the unknown won't seem as daunting. For example, how do you learn to manage a team? By managing a team. Don't get into a thought error of declining an opportunity because you have never done it. Of course you haven't, but you'll learn. Don't be afraid to step out of your comfort zone and gain new skills through experience.

Continuous participation in learning will provide you with a great lever as you age, as compared with people who stop learning as soon as they get out of school. You might think working at a job is learning, but unless you are actively challenging your processes, roles, and interactions, you are stagnating. Repeating the same task for twenty years does not automatically make you more efficient than your coworker who has been doing it for three years, unless you have put your brain into your work and have been engaged in learning.

Moreover, be open to new ways of doing a task, as this can lead to improvements in efficiency and effectiveness. Try new methods even if they seem unconventional. Experimentation is key to this process as it allows for the testing and exploration of different approaches—by constantly looking for new ways to do a task, individuals and organizations can stay ahead of the curve. Evaluate the results of your experimental techniques to identify what works and what doesn't, then make informed decisions about how to move forward.

Don't be afraid to take a calculated risk. Your idea might turn out to be inefficient, but you learned something along the way. You probably will get an even better idea at the end.

Also, things that might not have worked five years ago might just be the answer today. Life changes, and you change too.

Learn about personal growth. The more you can manage

your mind, the easier it will be to get out of your comfort zone and do scary things. When you have a better control over your thoughts, you then get a better control over your actions.

For example, if you believe no one would be interested in the book you want to write, it will be hard to get yourself to sit down and dedicate hours to this project. To increase your motivation, try a more hopeful thought, like, "If one person gets value out of my teaching, it will be worth it." You could also entertain the idea that maybe the book will sell.

Continuing education is key when striving for success in any field. Learning helps you stay ahead of your peers and grow professionally faster than those who don't invest time in themselves. Make sure each day brings something new that challenges and inspires growth for both you and those around you. Continual learning is one of the most valuable investments one can make.

Chapter 21 - Write Faster

I f you are serious about being more productive in the office, one of the easiest and most efficient ways to do this is by learning to type faster. Typing with ten fingers can be up to ten times faster than typing with two, and it will save you a lot of hours over the course of your career. From emails and reports to brainstorming sessions and presentations, knowing how to type quickly and accurately can make all the difference in your ability to get things done more quickly. Don't tell me your one-finger typing is awesome and really fast. It's not. Don't fool yourself.

Learn the right typing technique. Proper finger placement on the keyboard can help increase your speed. There are plenty of websites that teach you how to type, such as Typing.com or 10FastFingers.com, and software programs such as Typing-Master, RapidTyping, and Typing Tutor. A couple of hours invested in this type of learning will save you so much during your career. Practice regularly. Aim to increase not only the speed but also the accuracy. I know of people who can type but have to delete so often that it slows them down. You might want to try online typing tests that can help you measure your speed and identify areas for improvement.

Next, learn how to use keyboard shortcuts. Many programs,

such as Microsoft Word, have groups of keys that can be used to perform common tasks such as copying and pasting text. The ones I use most often are: Ctrl+X (cut text); Ctrl+Z (cancel the last input); Ctrl+Y (redo the last delete); Ctrl+C (copy); and Ctrl+V (paste). Try them! You will save time.

Make sure your keyboard is comfortable to use and is at the correct height and angle to reduce the chances of you getting tired or developing pain in your fingers, wrists, or arms.

Many people are turning to dictation applications or software that can help them type faster by allowing them to convert spoken words to text. There are free options included in Word and Google Docs, or you can buy Dragon Speech Recognition. I have been using the Google Voice option on my phone, and the accuracy is satisfying.

Learning how to type faster is an invaluable skill that anyone who uses computers regularly should master if they want to get more done in the workplace. Investing some time in improving your typing skills will pay dividends down the road when it comes to getting tasks completed efficiently.

Chapter 22 - Document

No matter how high up the ladder you climb, documenting business processes is crucial and can help you be more effective. Writing down the steps needed to accomplish a task will help you see it clearly in your mind. Once the process is on paper, you might identify bottlenecks in your workflow and make changes to improve overall efficiency. Clear and detailed process documentation can help ensure that everyone involved has a clear understanding of his or her responsibilities and how the process works.

Moreover, if your process is documented, you may delegate it to anyone. This will allow a coworker to take over during vacations or sick days so that your work is done when you get back.

New employees can more easily learn their roles by reviewing process documentation. They won't need to ask you questions as most of the answers will be available in writing. Also, it just makes sense to leave your position with all the tools in place for your replacement. Documenting processes is a good practice in the workplace, helping to ensure continuity in the event of employee turnover or unexpected disruptions.

Documenting also allows you to keep track of how to do

regular tasks that you only execute every so often. Instead of having to figure it out each time, you can quickly refer to your step-by-step methodology. This not only makes it faster but also ensures quality as it reduces the room for error. You won't forget key activities when you can refer to a record of the tasks that must be completed and in which order. You won't need to rely on your memory and hope for the best, all the while running the risk of having to go back to fix something.

As an example, I documented the process of self-publishing my books. On the checklist are the steps to successfully add the content online, update my website, and launch the book. It saves me a lot of time and guesswork.

Decide where you will keep track of your processes. You can use your current processes to build others, so the more you document, the easier it gets. Keep your documentation organized.

I also recommend building packing lists if you have to travel for work. When I had to go on the road to visit customers, I used my checklist every single time I needed to pack. If I forgot an item, I added it to the list for the next trip. I could pack in minutes. You can build a checklist for camping or for other activities that require luggage.

One last tip—save frequently used websites to your browser's Favorites or Bookmarks tab. This allows you to easily access the website without having to manually type in the URL or use a search engine to find it. To save a website to your favorites in Chrome, click on the star at the right side of the URL bar. You can also use the keyboard shortcut Ctrl+D on Windows or Cmd+D on Mac to save the website to your favorites. Once the website is saved, you can easily access it by clicking the Favorites or Bookmarks tab in your browser. Additionally, you can organize your bookmarks in a folder and title it for easy identification.

Any time you spend documenting will come back to you tenfold. No matter what kind of tasks you have on your plate, experiment to optimize all the steps. Build and refine your processes to increase speed of completion.

Chapter 23 - Get the Right Tools

The proper tools make all the difference in any job. Whether you're a student, a manager, or even a construction worker, having the right tools can make your job easier and more efficient.

For office workers, a powerful computer is a necessity. The faster your computer is, the better it is at performing multiple programs at once. Make sure that you have a reliable and up-to-date system that can handle large amounts of data and heavy software. This will help speed up your workflow and allow you to be more productive with less downtime waiting for programs to open or processes to finish.

Reliable high-speed internet is also essential if you use your computer for work or study. A slow internet connection can lead to hours wasted while you wait for pages to load or downloads to finish, which can significantly reduce productivity. Investing in high-speed internet will save you time and money in the long run.

If part of your job requires spending a lot of time on the phone, a headset will be worth the investment. Not only does a headset allow you to keep both hands free while talking, but it also helps improve sound quality by reducing background noise as well as blocking out external noises from other people or devices around you. A headset also reduces neck strain caused by holding up a phone for extended periods, so you will be able to have long conversations without getting tired too quickly.

Don't waste energy on broken tools—repair them or replace them. The expense may not seem worth it, but working with faulty equipment can take away from valuable time that could have been used elsewhere if everything was functioning properly. Replacing defective items will help ensure that tasks are completed with minimal hassle. I laugh when I see coworkers getting frustrated with a useless pen but still putting it back in the penholder. They'll get mad repeatedly instead of taking two seconds to trash the pen.

Storing tools according to how often they are used is another important step toward increasing efficiency. For example, you can store frequently used tools such as pens, markers, and scissors on top of desks rather than keeping them in drawers, where they may be forgotten about until needed again, at which point you would waste precious minutes looking for them. Keep in a drawer the tools you use monthly, and store the things you rarely need somewhere else in the office. If you don't use a stapler, there's no need to decorate your desk with it. I like to keep my desk clutter-free and organized.

For tasks where you must request a signature, obtain approval, write your address, or identify products, consider purchasing an ink pad to save time. Alternatively, question whether the work is necessary or done in the most streamlined way. While some employers have policies that can't be altered, there may be tasks they are more open to eliminating. Cutting unnecessary repetitious activities can free up valuable time and energy.

Banking online offers a wide range of options, from transferring money to paying bills to investing in different types of accounts. You can even deposit checks and make additional mortgage payments, all while sitting at home. Embrace online banking to simplify your financial management and save time.

Finally, investing in powerful software can pay off. MS Word proofing tools, for example, can help catch spelling and grammar errors, allowing for clearer and more professional communication. Additionally, the right software can also help you automate monotonous tasks and streamline workflow, leaving time for more important tasks. Overall, these well-chosen investments can help improve productivity, accuracy, and success in business and personal endeavors.

When it comes down to it, making sure you have the right tools will help ensure that everything gets done as efficiently as possible. With the right setup and organization, anyone can become more productive with daily tasks.

Chapter 24 - Free Your Mind

Your brain can only hold a specific quantity of information. So if you weigh it down with lists to remember, its power for thinking creatively will be reduced. It will only be processing menial information, losing the opportunity to operate at its full capacity.

Methods for freeing your mind from this mess can be a key to improving your effectiveness. When I talk about freeing your mind, I am not referring to meditation. I am referring to the various tasks and responsibilities that occupy your thoughts, such as household chores, upcoming meetings, personal projects, home renovations, car troubles, and calls to Grandma.

There is a way to collect these thoughts in one place and organize them for future use so they don't live rent-free in your brain anymore. Start by experimenting with some of my recommendations and adjust as you go.

I use Google Keep to maintain lists online. I have a shared grocery list with my husband. If I notice an item goes missing, I add it to the list right away. I also have a list of stores I go to regularly, and I add items as I think of them. Therefore, I know exactly what I need to buy the next time I have to go to the mall. I don't have to hope I'll remember and come back with half the items my family needed. It saves us a lot of time.

I also recommend creating an idea bank. Organize it as simply as possible just to get started. You will refine as you go. The benefits are numerous. For starters, an idea bank helps keep your mind organized as all your thoughts are neatly tucked away in one place rather than scattered about in various places. This will ensure that none of them are lost or forgotten. It serves as a great resource for future projects—you can always refer to the bank for inspiration or guidance on how to move forward. Finally, keeping an idea bank helps boost creativity as it encourages you to think outside the box and come up with fresh new ideas.

Getting started doesn't have to be complicated. All you need is somewhere to store all your ideas—this could be anything from a notebook or journal to an app on your phone. If you prefer physical storage options, notebooks like Moleskine are great for keeping track of daily thoughts, while apps like Evernote are perfect for digital storage. From there, it's just a matter of writing down any thoughts that come into your head so they don't slip away. Review these ideas periodically. Put them on the to-do list if applicable and purge and add as you go.

Chapter 25 - Spread Your Tentacles

In the corporate world, a good reputation and strong professional relationships can be incredibly valuable. When people know you and appreciate your work, they are more likely to think of you when opportunities arise. This can include promotions, new projects, or even job opportunities. Building a strong professional network takes time and effort, but it can pay off in the long run.

Your good reputation also helps to establish trust and credibility with your colleagues and supervisors. When people know and respect you, they are more likely to believe in your abilities and give you more responsibility.

Connect with people from all levels within the organization, regardless of their position on the corporate ladder. By doing so, you can gain valuable insights and knowledge from different departments, which can be essential to making informed decisions and solving complex problems. Network during your lunch break. Since everyone must eat, you might as well take that opportunity to build relationships. Also, try taking part in company team-building activities and attending networking events.

Additionally, forming personal relationships with your colleagues makes it easier to approach them when you need help or have questions. When people know and appreciate you, they are more likely to be willing to help you in your career. They might provide mentorship, give you feedback, or even make introductions that could lead to new opportunities.

So make yourself known to your colleagues. Attend company events, join social clubs, or chat with your coworkers during breaks. In short, creating a diverse network of colleagues can lead to numerous benefits, including access to critical information, a better understanding of the organization, and a support system to rely on in times of need.

An easy way to build trust with your colleagues is to be helpful and offer value to them. Share useful information or resources. This can help establish you as a knowledgeable and trustworthy person, which can lead to even stronger connections and professional-growth opportunities.

For example, if you come across a report that relates to a project your colleague is working on, take the time to share it with them. If you have expertise in a certain area, offer to help with any questions or challenges they may be facing. By providing value to your coworkers, you not only help them succeed, but you also build your own reputation as a team player and an asset to the organization.

Investing time in small talk with those who enjoy social interaction can help build relationships and create a positive work environment. However, it's important to recognize that not everyone enjoys socializing and to be mindful of their body language. Respect their boundaries and do not force conversation if they seem uninterested.

While small talk may not be everyone's favorite activity, it can be a useful tool for connecting with people and gathering information. If you find it difficult to initiate a conversation, consider preparing a few simple phrases that will help you make contact. A question I often use during social activities is, "What brought you to this conference?" This phrase helps me break the ice.

Maintaining a positive attitude can have a significant impact on your work. People are naturally drawn to those who exhibit enthusiasm and energy, as that attitude creates a more pleasant and productive atmosphere. Being positive can help to boost morale and create a supportive atmosphere, which can lead to better collaboration and stronger relationships with colleagues.

There are several ways to cultivate a positive outlook, including focusing on the good things in your life, practicing gratitude, and finding joy in the small things. You can also try to reframe negative situations and find the silver lining in challenging experiences.

In the workplace, it's important to display positivity not only in your interactions with colleagues but also in your approach to tasks and projects. Focus on solutions instead of problems, take on challenges with a can-do attitude, and find ways to make the work enjoyable. By doing so, you will make the work environment more pleasant and increase your job satisfaction.

Overall, building strong professional relationships and a good reputation in the corporate world is essential for career success. It can open doors to new opportunities, establish trust, and provide support along the way, allowing you to reach your goals faster.

Chapter 26 - Manage Data Inflows

We all know we can get buried under emails, articles to read, and information to process.

Organized and easily accessible data inflow is crucial to increasing your productivity because it reduces the time and effort spent searching for information. This allows you to focus on tasks that require your attention.

Efficient management of incoming data also improves decision-making. When data is organized, it's easier for you to analyze it and make informed choices. This can lead to better choices. Moreover, it helps team members work together and collaborate effectively, which leads to better communication and improved outcomes.

Efficient data management can make people feel calmer and less overwhelmed. Conversely, a cluttered and disorganized data system can cause confusion and frustration, leading to increased stress levels.

To better manage data inflows, you might want to try implementing the TRAF system. It stands for Toss, Refer, Act, and File. Here's a brief explanation of each step.

- Toss. The first step is to review your documents and trash what is not relevant, duplicates, or useless. Getting rid of these documents frees up space and reduces clutter, making it easier to focus on what's important.

- Refer. Next, consider any document that someone else should take care of. This will help you lighten your workload and make better use of your time.
- Act. For tasks that can't be tossed or referred, you need to act. Decide on the most important task and begin working on it or schedule it on your agenda. Prioritizing is crucial.
- File. Once a task is complete, file the relevant information and materials in an organized manner. This makes it easier to access and reduces your risk of losing important details. Create a clear filing system for your emails and for your office documents. Clean your system once a year to get rid of older documents.

A common daily challenge is to manage emails and mail effectively. There are many techniques that can help you sort through them.

- Set up a system for organizing emails. Create folders for different categories, such as work, personal, and action items. This makes it easier to find specific emails and keep your inbox organized. However, don't be scared to use the delete button most of the time. Once you have processed a task, you probably won't need to keep traces, unless you might get sued.
- Unsubscribe from unnecessary emails. Regularly unsubscribe from emails that are no longer relevant or important. This will reduce the amount of incoming mail and make it easier to deal with the messages that matter. If you don't read the newsletter, don't let it enter your inbox. Block any

repeat senders of junk mail.

- Use filters. Set up filters to automatically route emails to specific folders, based on criteria such as sender, subject, or keywords. This saves time and reduces the number of emails you will need to manually sort.

- Respond promptly. Answer emails as soon as possible, or at least within a day or two. This shows that you value the sender's time and helps to build strong relationships. Touch it once—read, decide, act. Don't open and read if you don't have time to answer.

- Use templates. Create templates for common emails, such as responses to frequently asked questions or follow-up messages. This saves time and helps to ensure that all emails are consistent in tone and content. You can even create content on an FAQ page to prevent these emails from coming to you in the first place.

- Manage physical mail. Sort physical mail as soon as it arrives, throwing away unnecessary items and filing important documents in a designated place. This helps to keep your workspace organized and reduces clutter.

Writing the perfect email can be a challenge. Keeping your email answers short and focused on one topic is an effective way to communicate. When writing an email, try to be concise and to the point. Avoid writing lengthy explanations or including multiple topics in one email, as this can make it difficult for the recipient to understand and respond. If the recipient is confused, you run the risk of waiting longer for a response.

If you find that your email response is growing longer than five sentences, consider making a phone call instead. A phone call allows for real-time communication and can often be a more efficient way to resolve complex or sensitive issues.

Keeping your email answers short saves your recipient time since they can quickly understand the purpose and respond without having to wade through a lengthy message. This will keep them from asking you to rephrase.

Experiment with some of those methods and soon you will notice how much simpler managing data inflows has become.

Chapter 27 - Delegate

Delegating is a great way to get things done more efficiently and can also be beneficial for developing people's skills. Assigning tasks to other people is a key part of any successful team. However, it is not always easy and requires careful consideration of who will be best suited to take on each task. Here are a few tips on how to delegate effectively.

Start by understanding the strengths and weaknesses of your team. You should know what they like doing and what they're good at so that you can assign tasks accordingly. This will ensure that the tasks are being completed in the most efficient manner possible.

Also, training is an invaluable investment of time when it comes to delegation. Not only does it help people master the necessary skills, but it also shows your team members that you care about their success and are willing to spend time helping them learn new things. This will yield long-term benefits in terms of productivity as well as employee morale.

So while training prior to delegating might be necessary, new tasks are also training opportunities for your team members. When you delegate, you are helping them become better at their jobs and more knowledgeable in their fields. This can go a long way in building trust and loyalty within your team as well as increasing overall efficiency.

Constantly micromanaging or freaking out over every small problem can lead to increased stress levels for both you and your team members, so try not to be too hard on yourself or them—everyone makes mistakes. Accept that if the overall results are good, it doesn't matter how they got them. By trusting others enough to give them tasks, you are showing respect and allowing them room to grow within their roles—which ultimately leads to better performance from each team member.

Delegate at home too. Assigning age-appropriate chores to your children will not only encourage them to help out around the house but can also benefit their development. They learn responsibility and gain a sense of accomplishment from completing their assigned tasks, which can build self-confidence and pride. For example, kids should be responsible for putting away their toys. They also can set the table, feed the pets, and water the plants. Make sure you select tasks that are right for their ages and abilities. By delegating simple chores, you can help your kids build character.

There are also online platforms, such as Upwork and Fiverr, that connect freelancers with customers all over the world. So you can delegate certain tasks on a more or less regular basis.

You can also take advantage of advances in artificial intelligence. You can use AI tools to draw plans, schedule meetings, conduct research, and even write reports or articles. By delegating these tasks to high-performance AI systems, you can optimize your productivity and achieve results more efficiently.

Delegation is an important skill for any leader or manager and is easy if done correctly. It can be beneficial on many levels, both personal and professional.

Chapter 28 - Manage Your Emotions

Negative emotions can derail your good intentions. Managing your feelings increases your efficiency because it lets you maintain a clear and focused state of mind. Emotional regulation means controlling your reactions to stressful and challenging situations, thereby reducing the impact of frustration, anger, or anxiety. When you are in control of your emotions, you are less likely to become distracted or overwhelmed, which allows you to concentrate on the task at hand, make better decisions, and prioritize your work more effectively.

Facing your emotions and acting despite them can be key factors in personal and professional growth. When we avoid feeling bad, we often waste time worrying, procrastinating, or engaging in self-doubt and negative self-talk. This not only slows us down and reduces our productivity, but it can also limit our potential for success. On the other hand, when we learn to face our fears, we develop a growth mindset, become more confident, and are better equipped to tackle challenges that come our way.

By acting in the face of negative emotions, you gain experience that can help you with similar challenges in the future. For example, getting a bad review on a book is devastating the first time, but as your sales grow, you will inevitably get more of them as your work will not be for everyone. Persevering despite the negative emotions associated with criticism is essential to progress.

When we work through our emotions, we develop the ability to bounce back from setbacks, which can be a valuable skill in both personal and professional contexts. Additionally, taking action can allow us to reframe emotions as a motivator rather than a limiting factor, helping us build momentum toward achieving our goals.

Another feeling that needs to be managed is discouragement. Many factors can cause it, such as monotony, lack of recognition, heavy workload, conflicts with colleagues or superiors, unrealistic goals, insufficient pay, or a hostile work environment. By recognizing and addressing the sources of negativity and frustration that arise during work, we mitigate their impact. This can involve taking breaks when necessary, reframing negative thoughts, asking for help, talking to a trusted friend, and finding ways to stay positive and motivated.

Even though negative emotions are a normal part of human life, by raising your awareness of what you are feeling, you can recognize what is happening and use self-care wisely.

Chapter 29 - Act Scared

In the previous chapter, we explored the concept of emotions and their impact on our lives. However, one emotion deserves a special mention—fear. It has the power to consume us and steal our dreams if we allow it to. It is often the primary emotion that arises when we are faced with critical decisions or the need to take important action.

Fear is an essential human emotion that helps protect us from danger. It triggers our natural fight-or-flight response, which can be useful in certain situations. However, when fear becomes overwhelming and irrational, it can be debilitating and hold us back from reaching our full potential.

Fear can manifest in different ways, such as anxiety, worry, stress, and panic. It can arise from various sources, including experiences, uncertainty about the future, or self-doubt. It is often easier to give in to this emotion than to confront the challenges we face. Acting in the face of fear is the first step toward success.

Yes, it's scary to leave a job.

Yes, it's scary to invest in an online course.

Yes, it's scary to ask for help.

Yes, it's scary to move to another country.

Yes, it's scary to make offers.

Yes, it's scary to go live on social media.

Yes, it's scary to make that phone call.

What is that one action you've been procrastinating on because of fear?

Letting fear control our actions will only hinder our success. Overcoming it is crucial if we are to realize our full potential. Fear often causes us to hesitate. Taking action despite these feelings is essential to building resilience and courage. When we push ourselves to act outside of our comfort zones, we can develop new skills and strengthen our ability to overcome obstacles. The more we practice confronting what scares us, the more courageous we become, and the more likely we are to succeed in the face of adversity.

Remember, fear is a natural human emotion, and everyone experiences it. The difference between those who succeed and those who don't is their willingness to act. When we choose to face our fears, we gain confidence in our abilities, and we begin to see challenges as opportunities rather than obstacles.

A way to overcome fear is to reframe our thoughts and to focus on the positive outcomes from taking action. By shifting our mindset, we can view fear as an opportunity for personal growth.

To be efficient and productive, we must prioritize the tasks that have the most significant impact, even if they are scary. Confronting our fears is essential to building resilience and courage. By doing things that scare us, we can develop new skills, overcome obstacles, and achieve our goals.

Section Two - Multitasking the Right Way

Multitasking can be detrimental to productivity and performance because it forces the brain to constantly switch between activities, causing cognitive overload and leading to a decreased ability to focus on each individual task. Additionally, multitasking often results in errors and decreased quality of work and can increase stress and mental exhaustion. Research has shown that it is more effective to focus on one task at a time and complete it before moving on to the next one.

But what if you chose tasks that could be combined without requiring you to switch at all? The key is to pick ones that can be done simultaneously.

The objective is to create synergies and achieve faster results by combining and optimizing your various goals and tasks. By finding ways to blend important tasks together, you can maximize your time, resources, and energy.

To use this technique, you might need to innovate. For instance, taking care of the kids and cleaning can be combined into a fun and interactive experience, such as a dance-cleaning party. This approach not only allows you to accomplish two tasks at once but also adds an element of joy to what might have been a mundane chore. However, no matter how creative you are, keep in mind that some tasks may still be unpleasant.

I will provide you with many examples later, but an easy one is to work out with your kids. Try not to compartmentalize your life and instead create synergies between your various roles. You could combine exercise and leisure by going for a walk or run in a scenic area, or you could mix work and socializing by scheduling a virtual coffee break with a colleague. This approach helps you to make the most of your time so you can reach your goals sooner and with greater satisfaction. By blending various priorities, you get double the results in the same amount of time. Finishing your work faster will free your time so you can later enjoy the company of your kids or sit down to quietly sip a cup of tea.

Freeing up your time can have a profound impact on your ability to nurture yourself. Self-care is an essential aspect of maintaining good mental, physical, and emotional health. Use this extra free time to meditate, exercise, read, or simply relax. Additionally, you can pursue hobbies and interests that bring you joy and fulfillment. I'd like to give back more freedom to each of you.

Combining activities can also help you effectively complete important tasks. For example, many people struggle to maintain an active lifestyle due to limited time and a busy schedule. However, as you will see in the coming chapters, by incorporating exercise into other aspects of your routine, you can make it a more manageable and integral part of your daily life.

The *Double Your Time* mindset is so powerful that I must warn you—this productivity technique can be dangerous if used all the time. It will wear you down. But if you use it properly with the right energy management, you will be able to get much more done. Knowing I can manage my time allows me to be more efficient when I work and at peace those moments when I want to be fully present.

In the following chapters, I provide you with many ideas of ways to combine and create synergies between tasks and activities. My goal is to offer ideas of areas where you can double your productivity. The point is to try it out for yourself and see if it works for you. Some suggestions will be more helpful than others. Don't get caught in the examples. I expect you to find ideas of your own to benefit your lifestyle.

Chapter 1 - At Home

As parents, we might feel obligated to attend to all our children's demands, slaving to clean up after them and fetch them snacks. I can certainly relate to this. In an attempt to simplify my children's lives and make things more convenient for them, I often find myself serving them. While it may feel easier in the short term to comply with a request, it creates long-term challenges. This type of behavior can foster their sense of entitlement and dependence as well as undermining their ability to take care of themselves and develop important life skills. It's important to strike a balance between providing support and allowing them to learn and grow through experience and responsibility. Serving them now is a future disservice to them. The job of parents is to coach their children and teach them how to be autonomous humans so they can be independent and proud.

Therefore, you can shamelessly get your kids to help. There are many charts online showing what tasks are appropriate for each age. Anything you manage to make them do you won't have to do yourself.

You could plan on a time to hurry through the cleaning together then reward yourselves by doing something fun together, such as playing a video game or doing a puzzle. If you work from home or are a self-employed entrepreneur, integrating your kids into your work can be a valuable learning experience for them. You can share your values, work ethic, and passion, helping them to develop important skills that will serve them throughout their lives. They will feel valued and important when they are able to assist you in your work, pretending to write a book on a broken keyboard, drawing pictures for customers, or greeting clients at the office. This not only lets you continue your work but also provides an educational opportunity for your children, allowing them to grow and learn in a supportive and engaging environment. They will cherish the memories, and so will you!

Here are some other ideas to get you started doubling your time with your kids, depending on their age and abilities.

- Cook with your kids. Cooking helps children develop important life skills, such as measuring, counting, following recipes, and preparing food. It encourages them to try new foods and develop healthy eating habits, which can have long-lasting benefits for their health and wellness. Although it can be challenging at times, cooking together can also be a fun and engaging way for families to bond.
- Go grocery shopping together. Going grocery shopping with kids can offer numerous benefits for both children and parents. It teaches kids about budgeting, nutrition, and meal planning, which are important life skills. Buying groceries involves counting, comparing prices, and calculating budgets, which can help kids develop their math skills. It encourages decision-making and critical thinking as kids figure out what to buy.
- Gardening. Working in the garden can help kids develop

a healthy lifestyle and improve their physical and mental well-being. They will spend time outside, encouraging their interest in taking care of our planet. They will learn patience while their seeds are slowly growing. Gardening is a great way to learn about science and nature while developing an appreciation for healthy food.

- House chores. Doing chores with kids teaches them about all the tasks that are required to keep the house clean and organized. By completing chores successfully, kids get a sense of accomplishment that boosts their self-esteem. They have the satisfaction of contributing to the well-being of the entire family by being responsible and following through on tasks.

- House maintenance. If you are a homeowner, there always seems to be something to fix. Ask your kid for assistance. For example, they could fetch tools, measure, or hold the ladder. Not only will you benefit from their help, but they will gain confidence in their ability to tackle household projects. Letting kids help is a great opportunity to improve teamwork and communication skills while bonding and saving money and can help them appreciate the hard work that goes into maintaining a home. When we remodeled the bathroom, the kids had a blast destroying the ceramic tiles.

Can you think of other ways to turn a tedious chore into a fun bonding activity with your kids?

Lastly, if you're trying to reduce your TV time but your partner is still glued to the screen, don't worry. You can still spend time together by cuddling up with a book or taking an online class with earbuds. This way, you can be in the same space but still engage in different activities that are fulfilling and enjoyable for both of you.

Chapter 2 - At Work

It's natural to have periods of downtime at work, especially once we have our tasks under control and have become more efficient. We need to make the most of these opportunities by finding a way to add value to our work or pursue our goals and passions.

While it's tempting to spend this time checking social media or chatting with coworkers, it's much more productive to use it for self-improvement or to pursue personal interests. This could be learning a new skill, working on a side project, or simply taking a break to recharge and clear your mind. The key is to make the most of the time and use it in a way that is beneficial and fulfilling.

Using downtime or lunch breaks, you can get many different personal tasks done. Here are a few ideas to get you started.

- Short errands. You can gas your car or pick up groceries.
- Quick tasks. You can make reservations, order online, pay bills, email your customers and prospects for your side business, or book doctors' appointments. If you work from home, you can start a load of laundry, empty the dishwasher, or fold clothes.
- Learning. You can use this time to continue your education

by reading a book, taking an online course, or watching educational videos on a subject that you're interested in.

- Hobbies. You can pursue a personal hobby or interest. For example, you could write, draw, journal, or work on a craft project. This is easier if you work from home.
- Exercise. You could go for a walk, do some stretches, or practice a mindfulness exercise like meditation or yoga. Bonus points if you exercise with your colleagues, allowing you to network at the same time.
- Relaxation. Finally, it's important to use your break time to simply relax and recharge. This could mean taking a nap, reading a fiction book, or listening to music.

Remember to use this time to prioritize your own needs and well-being. Trust me, it's incredible how quickly these little baby steps taken in the short time slots will add up. If your brain needs to recharge, instead of drifting away on social media, get up and deliver papers or other things that you must get off your desk. That lets you enjoy a little time off yet still get something done.

There are other ways to increase your productivity at your job. If you work on the road, you can return phone calls during your commute. What other tasks could you combine?

Chapter 3 - In the Kitchen

Most of the time in the kitchen is spent on activities like cooking, preparing meals, cleaning, organizing, and storing food. Whether or not you enjoy those necessary tasks, there are ways to combine them for maximum efficiency.

First, incorporate meal prepping to reduce the time you spend in the kitchen. Meal prepping is the process of planning, preparing, and portioning out meals in advance, typically for a week or several days at a time. The goal of meal prepping is to have healthy, convenient meals available for consumption, which can help people save time and make healthier food choices.

If being with your kids is one of your priorities, get them involved in the kitchen. If you are patient enough, this can be a fun and educational experience for both you and them.

Even small children can participate in kitchen activities such as stirring ingredients or washing fruits and vegetables. Older kids can be responsible for more complex tasks, such as measuring ingredients, cracking eggs, or following a recipe.

While it may take a bit more time to involve your kids in the kitchen, you are teaching them invaluable skills and spending quality time with them, all while cooking a delicious meal for your family. That's triple action!

Here are more ideas for combining tasks in the kitchen.

- While washing the dishes, use a speech-to-text app to write your blog, return personal phone calls, or chat with your family.
- While cooking, use any spare time to empty the dishwasher, wipe down the counters, chop vegetables for later meals, or prepare tomorrow's lunch.

The key is to make the most of any waiting period by completing small tasks that can be done efficiently in the kitchen. By combining activities, you can minimize downtime and maximize efficiency, allowing you to spend more time on what really matters.

Chapter 4 - In the Bathroom

There are a few tips and hacks that can help you make the most of your bathroom routines. First, invest in the right tools. Using high-quality products, such as a good razor or a fast-drying towel, can make your bathroom routine faster and more effective.

One time-consuming task for parents is having to watch little kids when they bathe. There are many things that you can get done while they play in the water. I used to fold clothes right next to them while we talked. You could also go over some homework with them, for example, quizzing them about math, spelling, or history. That way, your child gets clean and learns at the same time. You could also make good use of this time by cleaning the sink and toilet or wiping down the counters.

Some parents have a shower routine, in which the little ones shower with a parent. If that feels comfortable for both of you, it could save you a lot of time.

Here are a few other ideas for combining tasks in the bathroom.

- While waiting for the shower to warm up, wipe down the shower walls.
- While waiting for hair conditioner to work, shave your legs,

wash your body, or apply a face mask.

- While waiting for your nail polish to dry, read a book, watch an online training course, or listen to a podcast.
- While using the bathroom, check and respond to emails or messages on your phone. My husband often talks to his parents during that time, and I'm taking German lessons using an app.

What can you try for yourself? Do you have other ideas on how to use your downtime in the bathroom? Remember, the key is to identify small tasks that can be done efficiently in the bathroom while you're already there. By combining tasks, you can free up time for other activities throughout the day.

Chapter 5 - Exercising

For many people, exercise is the first thing to get dropped from their busy schedules. When time is tight, it's easy to procrastinate and put off working out. After all, skipping one day doesn't seem like a big deal, and it's easy to convince yourself that you'll have more time tomorrow.

Unfortunately, life doesn't function that way. Time is a finite resource, and you need to make a conscious effort to incorporate movement into your daily routine. Even small actions can make a big difference, so don't worry about fancy workouts or following the latest fitness trends. Just aim to move your body a little bit every day, even if it's just a short walk around your neighborhood. Set the bar low so you have no excuse not to follow through.

If you're short on time, the best way to ensure that you exercise is to make it a part of your daily schedule. Even if you can't fit in a single long workout, breaking it up into smaller sessions throughout the day can still provide plenty of benefits. Experts recommend that adults aim for at least one hundred fifty minutes of moderate-intensity aerobic activity per week. If you spread that out over seven days, that equates to a minimum of twenty-one minutes of exercise per day.

If you're a parent, try gradually incorporating more physical activities into your family's routine. For example, one easy way to increase your family's physical activity is to take a walk with your kids. Walking side by side not only gets your bodies moving but also allows you to share a special moment together. There are many ways to make this activity enjoyable. You can talk about your day, discuss issues in their lives, or teach them about nature. It's a fun and educational way to exercise.

There are also many exercise programs that involve kids as an integral part of the movement. For example, some parents use their babies as weights or do yoga with their kids. A stroller can be a great tool, allowing you to walk, run, roller skate, or bike while entertaining your kids. Go hiking or swim at the beach. The possibilities are endless, so get creative and find activities that work for you and your family.

There are many other ways to combine tasks while exercising.

- While working out, listen to an e-book or podcast or watch educational content.
- Make cleaning the house more fun and active by turning on music and picking up the pace. Not only will you get your heart pumping, but you'll also finish the cleaning faster. It's a win-win!
- Do gardening—it's a great way to exercise while growing healthy food. To get your heart rate up, use gardening tools that require more physical effort, such as manual shears instead of an electric trimmer. This will help you to work your muscles and burn more calories.
- Use your lunch break to go for a walk or work out. I used to work near a cross-country skiing trail, and people would ski during lunch. How cool is that?
- Go outside to move. Get some fresh air and a dose of

vitamin D. Studies have shown that spending time in nature can help reduce symptoms of anxiety and depression.

- Walk everywhere you can. Walking provides many benefits, such as helping you maintain a healthy weight, strengthening your bones and muscles, increasing energy levels while reducing stress, and improving your sleep. You get your exercise, and you get to go places!

By incorporating exercise into your daily life, you maximize your time and make progress toward your health-and-fitness goals.

Chapter 6 - Cleaning

With the right mindset, cleaning can be a fun and energizing activity that contributes to your overall health and well-being. Cleaning and organizing can help reduce stress and anxiety by creating a sense of order and control. A tidy environment can also improve productivity and mental clarity, making it easier to focus on other activities.

I have already given examples of how you can combine cleaning with exercising, family time, or learning time. Here are a few other ideas.

- If you love watching TV, you could do other tasks at the same time, such as dusting or folding clothes.
- Use your ears. Turn on your favorite music, listen to an audiobook, learn something new, or stay up-to-date on the latest news and trends.
- Enjoy connections and strengthen your relationships with friends and family by catching up on the phone. Why not call your sister as you both do the dishes?
- Simply practice mindfulness by being present in the moment. Focus on the task at hand and pay attention to your thoughts and feelings.

By incorporating these activities into your cleaning routine, you can make the most of your time and energy and contribute to your overall well-being.

Chapter 7 - Commuting

Commuting is such a waste of time. Although getting rid of commuting entirely may not be feasible for everyone, there are some strategies to help you minimize it as much as possible. The first is to work remotely if your job allows for it, at least a few days a week. If working from home isn't an option, see if you can take public transportation instead of driving. This can reduce the stress of driving and save you money on gas and parking. If public transportation isn't available or convenient, try carpooling with coworkers who live nearby to get those same benefits. If you're able to, consider moving closer to your workplace or changing jobs. This could drastically reduce the time and expense of commuting. Depending on the distance between your home and workplace, you may be able to bike or walk, getting your exercise in at the same time. To make your trip faster and easier, negotiate a different schedule that allows you to avoid rush hour traffic.

Once you've exhausted all options for reducing or eliminating your daily commute, consider ways to make the most of the time you spend in your car.

Here are more ideas for combining tasks while commuting.

- While driving, you can chat with your kids, quiz them, or play an educational game such as counting numbers up or naming different types of birds.
- You could listen to a podcast or learn a new language.
- Alternatively, you can turn off all sounds and use this time to think, plan, be mindful, or brainstorm.

Moving Forward: Applying These Techniques in Your Life

Now that you have learned about twenty-eight simple techniques to jump-start your productivity and seven areas where you can multitask successfully, it's time to put them into practice. You may already be using some of these ideas, while others may be new to you. Don't be afraid to experiment and try new things.

Remember that everyone has a unique way of working and managing time, so what works for someone else may not work for you. Keep an open mind and be curious about how different techniques can help you improve your productivity and work more efficiently.

It's also important to remember that developing new habits and incorporating these techniques into your daily routine takes time and effort. Don't be discouraged if you don't see immediate results. Give yourself time to adjust and figure out what is best for you. Keep track of your progress and celebrate small successes along the way.

Ultimately, the goal is to find a balance. While being productive is important, it's equally important to take breaks, prioritize self-care, and avoid burnout. Use these techniques to help you work smarter, not harder, and create more time for the things that matter most to you.

Bonus Material

Looking to track your habits and stay on top of your goals? Our new worksheet is here to help! With space for up to six daily habits and seven months of tracking, it's the perfect tool to keep you accountable and motivated.

Simply print out the worksheet and start tracking your habits by putting a checkmark or writing down your progress each day. Whether you want to read more, exercise regularly, or even do one hundred jumping jacks a day, this worksheet will keep you on track.

But that's not all—you can even track your progress with specific numbers, such as the number of minutes you meditated or the number of miles you ran. It's completely customizable to suit your goals and preferences.

So what are you waiting for? Take the first step toward a better you and download our habit-tracking worksheet today!

Get it for free here: https://mailchi.mp/d7d6e72c9f20/habitcreationworksheet

About the Author

Josiane Fortin is a true expert in the field of productivity, having spent over twenty-five years honing her skills and perfecting her techniques. As a mother of two, a writer, a painter, a content creator, and a full-time worker, she knows how to get things done quickly and effectively.

With the valuable tips and strategies outlined in this book, Josiane has shared some of her best methods for maximizing efficiency. From eliminating distractions to utilizing time-saving tools, she offers a wealth of advice that can help you to do more in less time.

By following just a few of the methods outlined in this book, you too can experience a dramatic increase in your productivity. Whether you are a busy professional, a student, a parent, or anyone looking to improve their productivity, Josiane's techniques are sure to help you get more done in less time.

So why not take the first step toward a more productive and fulfilling life? Start implementing some of the strategies outlined in this book and see for yourself how much more you can accomplish in a day, a week, or even a year! With Josiane's expert guidance and support, you can achieve your goals and make the most of every moment.

www.ingramcontent.com/pod-product-compliance
Lightning Source LLC
LaVergne TN
LVHW050615200726
843508LV00010B/1861